UNLOCKED

A MANIFESTO ON LIVING TRUE

ART MCCRACKEN

UNLOCKED
A MANIFESTO ON LIVING TRUE
Copyright © 2024 by Art McCracken

To request permissions, contact the publisher at publish@joapublishing.com or choiceisthegift@gmail.com

Hardcover ISBN: 978-1-961098-70-1
Paperback ISBN: 978-1-961098-69-5
eBook ISBN: 978-1-961098-71-8
Printed in the USA.

Joan of Arc Publishing
Meridian, ID 83646
www.joapublishing.com

To the ones I love the most:

Melanie, Chyllia, Kensley, and Rylyn,

you are my reason.

TABLE OF CONTENTS

INTO THE UNKNOWN

"When life gets blurry, get to higher ground."

MOE

WHERE: 41°23'05.0"N 111°55'23.0"W

WHEN: October 19, 2012

WHO: Friends, Family, Colleagues, and My Conscience

As I step forward, I can feel the dirt under my feet as it grinds and shifts. I walk slowly to the base of what was so eloquently coined "the pamper pole." This pole is a 60-foot retired telephone pole, secured in a grove of tall pine trees on the side of a mountain. The pole has a ladder at its base that leans against its cold stature. Just beyond the top of the ladder is a handful of small u-shaped rungs that continue to lead up the pole. Atop this pole is a small weathered plywood disk, about the size of a medium pizza pan, that wobbles and spins and is the primary crux that must be navigated for someone with a mission of standing on top of the pole.

I'm harnessed and attached to two dynamic ropes that act as anchor points for protection and relief should something go wrong. Once you're on top of the pole, the objective is to stabilize yourself, catch your breath, take in the view, visualize the next phase of the challenge, and make the leap into the abyss of the canyon to a loosely suspended trapeze bar that hangs 75 feet off the ground and lies between the climber and the distant mountains. The hope is that you'll not only make the leap but then at the extent of your leap, you'll confidently catch the trapeze bar with your hands and experience a sense of accomplishment before you let go and let the ropes and harness catch you as you are lowered to the ground.

The illusion of the leap from the top of the pole on a hillside looking across a vast canyon makes the leap seem as if it is one into a void of mass depth.

For me, on this day, in this setting, on this weekend, with

friends and colleagues surrounding me and my family firmly affixed in my mind, I would make the leap.

This leap wasn't for the trapeze bar, and anyone who knows me well would know that I am eager for adventure. I've spent many years rock climbing and take no issue with heights or being roped in, precariously perched high above the ground. What people didn't know about me is that on that cool fall afternoon in the mountains northeast of Ogden, Utah, I was more frightened than I had ever been.

Thoughts of regret flooded my mind, as at the front of my mind I saw the filmstrip of those I loved. Up to that point in my life, I had lived much of life in full-on duplicity, hiding from those I loved. It was a life filled with darkness, betrayal, deceit, hypocrisy and ego; a life not well lived; a life with no honor to those I loved and served.

The top of this pole would represent a crossroad, if you will, between a life of self-service and a life of integrity and high service to others.

A choice.

I was broken, and yet I knew all along the life I had been choosing was never going to get me where I wanted to go. If there is one thing I had learned throughout my life it was this: if you run from the necessary change, it will chase you the rest of your life until you turn to face it head-on. Would I risk not making that choice that day and procrastinate the necessity of living true?

This was THE defining moment in my life.

Would I rise to the occasion, or would I let this retreat be another in my quiver of facilitated but not engaged?

It's as if my whole world was now in slow motion. There seemed to be no thought process for the obstacle but more an awareness of each breath. I could vividly imagine those I loved standing in front of me, almost begging for me to fight for them. I could see a life without guilt and selfishness. I could imagine living each day with integrity and high competency around the beliefs I held dear.

Experience mattered, and to this point my experience hadn't.

It was go time!

As I stepped to the base of the ladder and began ascending the pole, I felt the coolness of each rung on my hands as I slowly and almost arrogantly climbed the first section. I then tackled the small rungs bolted to the wood pole as I moved from 15 feet to 40 feet, and then another 10, bear-hugging the pole. I now stood on the last rung with one leg dangling while my hands began to navigate the spinning wooden disk atop the pole.

As I hugged the gnarled wooden surface, I shifted my body weight over the pole, and with a firm grip on the sides of the platform, I pushed and pulled my way to the top, where I slowly wobbled my way from a forward stretch with all fours affixed to the surface, to a couple of wobbling legs as my base of navigation for what lay ahead.

There it was—the trapeze bar—in front of me. I hadn't been too successful with the leap in times past, but something was different this time. I wasn't making the leap to leap, or to show others that I could. This leap was one of serious consequence and potential significance.

I could recall my dear friend, and co-facilitator, Travis advising on strategy for those attempting the leap from the top of the pole. He counseled participants to breathe, focus, envision, and then just do it. He also said that the fear of the leap can be mitigated if you'll focus on the two things you'd give your life's efforts for.

On this day my leap would prove to be a token of commitment toward living true.

I would be making this leap for my sweetheart and dear children.

I would be making this leap for those I served each day in my career and at home and those I had yet to serve.

Fully present was the choice to let go of a life of hypocrisy and selfishness and to dive headfirst into the unknown of consequence for my past.

I was fully aware and willing to take the risk.

I stood firmly on top of the pole in an eerie and haunting silence that shifted and overtook my body with a sense of calm and significance. I felt love. I could see clearly who I must serve and why I needed to make the leap. I had spent too many years held in contempt for what could be.

I peered into the distance and could see clearly the trapeze bar in front of me. It represented a new life. I could feel an energy and new strength for what could be should I decide that day to live true.

I leaned forward into the unknown and timed my jump with full momentum toward the bar. I can still feel the muscles of my thighs contracting as I pushed off of the wooden disk and flew through the air. I can still feel the athletic tape on my hands and shape of the bar that dangled in midair as I clenched my hands around its surface.

I made the leap!

I caught the bar!

My journey began . . .

What would unfold over the next 48 hours would be the start of a miracle that still lives today.

ARCHITECTURE

"Take thought for the future, and of the path ahead, by owning the decisions of the present."

MOE

I have spent the last 20 years of my career as a coach working with executives and business owners and their teams. More importantly, I've had the good fortune of being married to an incredible woman for almost 28 years and the blessing of being a father for much of that time as well.

It's been a hotbed of mistakes, both professionally and personally, along the way, and I am always forging forward in spite of the challenges this life affords me.

I have learned to serve this gift of mortality as a steward in my own home and in the lives of those I love and serve in my chosen career path.

You'll find I am not a fan of long, drawn out chapters. It's part of the reason behind the size of this book and brevity of each chapter.

I HAVE WRITTEN THIS BOOK FOR YOU IF . . .

you are a lost chaser of success; a corporate deviant with a stewardship beyond your present capability; a father, mother, parent, or friend with a conscience of high time. If you are someone who is committed to becoming better tomorrow than you were today, this book was written for you. For those who feel stuck, misaligned, hypocritical, disconnected, lost, and are willing to make a new committed effort to change the present result—this book was written for you. For those executives who have stopped wandering the halls of YOUR business, leaders who feel they have no place to turn for help—this book was written for you.

I can't say that any of the ideas in this book are new, per se. Are they relevant? Certainly, but mostly a reminder and a prick of the conscience in its grander sense for those who choose to turn the page. I believe that truth and knowledge are passed on from one generation to the next, with the intent to help serve those who will continue to build with that truth and knowledge long after we are gone.

Over the next several pages of this book, you'll be invited to take a familiar journey of opposing paradigms of both destruction and creation.

The ARCHITECTURE is deliberate.

There are seven LOCKED chapters and seven UNLOCKED chapters.

Within the LOCKED chapters, you'll find symptomatic descriptions of continued struggle and a tug-of war with life, and its varied circumstances. In many ways, it will represent a life of dissonance and duality. It is LOCKED and pained.

In the UNLOCKED chapters, you'll experience the opposite, and the symptomatic expressions that correspond with a new way of being—one of resonance and focused intent. These chapters will demonstrate a path of congruence to one's internal meter of truth and matters of significance.

Each chapter will end with either three REFLECTIONS (questions designed not just to have you look in the mirror but to help you shine the bright light of day on your own actions and existence) or three ACTION STEPS (meant to further develop your meaningful exchange with the world around you).

Each chapter heading contains a quote. Many of those are attributed to "MOE."

Who is MOE?

That's me. These are my own notions as I have tried to make sense of my own personal observations in life.

Therefore, MOE stands for just that: my own experience.

As you read, you will always have a choice: stagnancy or growth? Up or down? Judgment or curiosity? Time spent or time given? Fake it or face it?

LOCKED or UNLOCKED?

You'll also have a choice to decide when you'll flip the book and read it from perhaps another road even less traveled but one of truth and commitment beyond the charade.

I encourage you to take it at the pace most true to where you are today.

Perhaps you will let it challenge you in ways you've been procrastinating.

Wherever this road might lead you, I honor this part of your journey.

Some of the most impactful lessons I have learned along my way have been in the valley and point of choice to abandon an existence that could have only taken me to that point.

We've heard it said before that "the teacher appears when the student is ready." It was true for me in that crossroad moment atop the mountain, and continues to be to this day.

If there is one thing I know it is that as human beings we are hardheaded and adrift with ego.

Procrastination continues to be a form of stress relief and a decoy for those of us who give way to its enticing safety net.

You'll hear me talk often about honoring the gift.

What is the gift, you ask?

I believe the greatest gift in our mortal lives is the gift of CHOICE. How we honor that gift will shape the eternities.

My hope is that you'll not just see and hear the words but that you will feel the intent behind them and between them. I am grateful you are here. I have a reverence for your journey and for the growth you seek.

In short, my calling is people experience living true.

If you're ready to get to higher ground, if you're ready to unlock your highest and best self as you learn to honor those you love and serve, I invite you to turn the page so together we can take this journey.

Together, let's do the work of being better.

It's your time!

EGO

"You can only keep up the myth of your own importance for so long. If you don't break your ego, life will break it for you."[1]

JAY SHETTY

---

[1] Jay Shetty, *Think Like a Monk: Train Your Mind for Peace and Purpose Every Day*, (New York City: Simon and Schuster, 2020), 181.

One of our greatest challenges in life will be the dance with our own ego.

As humans, we have been conditioned over time to protect ourselves from danger, both physical and emotional.

We have a brain that is uniquely and importantly built to see what we want it to see and to gather quickly all the evidence that proves our position.

Whether it be an act of protecting ourselves from pain or uncomfortable exchanges with the world around us, or perhaps a quest to be seen as more visible and meaningful in the world we are trying to define, our ego stands ready to be our rescuer.

Ego is part and parcel to the drama in our lives, typically playing the character of "persecutor" with an angst and commitment to "be right."

How does Ego play out "in the arena?" It doesn't.

Ego is sidelined, and peanut gallery at best.

In Teddy Roosevelt's famous and often quoted passage from his speech, "Citizenship in a Republic," delivered at the Sorbonne on April 23, 1910, we see quite the opposite:

> It is not the critic who counts; not the man who points out how the strong man stumbles, or where the doer of deeds could have done them better. The credit belongs to the man who is actually in the arena, whose face is marred by dust and sweat and blood; who strives valiantly; who errs, who comes short again and again because there is no effort without

error and shortcoming; but who does actually strive to do the deeds; who knows great enthusiasms, the great devotions; who spends himself in a worthy cause; who at best knows in the end the triumph of high achievement, and who at worst, if he fails, at least fails while daring greatly, so that his place shall never be with those cold and timid souls who neither know victory nor defeat.

The "man in the arena" takes no interest in being the hero, martyr, or noble one without criticism and contender. He is simply in the arena, naked and striving to face the dragons of his own accord and existence.

As for the spectators: ego developed during times of abundance, if not curbed, will be the same ego that will shield our growth during times of scarcity.

This happens when we take an inappropriate amount of credit during the good times and readily point the finger in the bad times.

When our ego is turned up, we avoid feedback.

Paranoia will set in as you begin to believe that everything is about you, whether it be good or bad. Your concern and anxiousness for control of identity will begin to occupy your day.

We actually run from available feedback and do our best to insulate ourselves from the judgment or advice of someone else.

We believe we can do life on our own.

I see this play out inside companies and inside homes when leaders, peers, spouses, and parents believe they have to have all the answers and are unwilling to ask for help.

Some say EGO is an acronym for "Edging God Out."

> Because our ego craves positive attention, it can make us susceptible to manipulation. It makes us predictable. When people know this, they can play to our ego. When we're a victim of our own need to be seen as great, we end up being led into making decisions that may be detrimental to ourselves, our people, and our organization.[2]

When it comes to business, I love this poignant statement from Doug Stoddard: "A business that is not meeting its revenue projections, year after year, is hampered by a decision, somewhere along the way, that is attached to ego."[3]

The Stoics warned of ego ad nauseam, so much so that even one of the great authors of our time, Ryan Holiday, titled one of his seminal books on Stoicism *Ego is the Enemy.*

Ego has roots in identity fixation: "I want to be seen as . . ." or "I am unwilling to let go of what I want to be seen as."

Quick to pass judgment and to assume. We don't listen. We talk way too much.

---

[2]Rasmus Hougaard and Jacqueline Carter, "Ego Is the Enemy of Good Leadership," *Harvard Business Review*, November 6, 2018, https://hbr.org/2018/11/ego-is-the-enemy-of-good-leadership.

[3]Doug Stoddard, "Ego in Our Marketplaces," *Habit Breaker Weekly Tips* on LinkedIn, January 15, 2024, https://www.linkedin.com/pulse/ego-our-marketplaces-doug-stoddard-eqpic/.

We want more out of the world than we are willing to give to it.

Ego is FIXED- rather than GROWTH-oriented.

Narcissism.

Finger pointing.

Avoiding personal responsibility.

We give up easily and spew sour grapes when things don't go our way.

Command and control become the mark and tell of an egocentric leader who believes they are entitled to praise and compliance.

When ego is driving us, we will struggle with letting go and trusting anyone but ourselves.

This dance is a clunky one that leaves you partnerless at the end of the night.

Hamza Yusuf drew this conclusion: "The weak are dominated by their ego, the wise dominate their ego, and the intelligent are in constant struggle against their ego."[4]

Life is not an individual sport.

In case you haven't looked around in a while . . . you are surrounded by other human beings; they've just become invisible.

---

[4]Hamza Yusuf, co-founder of Zaytuna College, quoted on Zaytuna College (@ zaytunacollege) on X, June 8, 2018, 2:00 p.m., https://x.com/zaytunacollege/ status/1005177800360423426?lang=en.

3 REFLECTIONS

In what ways am I avoiding feedback?

_____

_____

_____

_____

_____

How often am I blaming others for our collective struggles?

_____

_____

_____

_____

Is my extension of trust tied to some elevated equation I have yet to define?

_____

_____

_____

_____

_____

ENTITLEMENT

"When you justify your own fears and doubts by repurposing them as an indifference toward others, the very thing you seek cannot be found."

MOE

When life doesn't go our way, we start to lose our patience with it.

When we lose our patience, we begin to see people as objects—easily dismissed and unimportant.

We begin to see the world and everyone in it as the issue, and our ploy to navigate the world as a solo act becomes highly visible to others.

Although, we don't do it entirely on our own. We continue to recruit an army of people who have come to our defense or at least given us rest in our mire. These individuals are not truly team members but rather means to an end, easily discarded when our bluff becomes less safe and secure in their hands. Oftentimes, this army shares characteristics of codependency and drama, making it a perfect match for more of the same.

It is a sickening place for those who watch it play out.

For those who are in it and working hard to maintain it, it is chaotic and empty.

When we get this way, we don't want to be seen by others as anything less than the façade we are trying to maintain, when in reality, much of the world around us sees brightly our arrogance and disconnect.

Humberto R. Maturana, Ph.D. said it best: "Blind to the transparency of our actions, we confuse the image we want to project with the being we want to bring forth."[5]

[5]Humberto Maturana with Francisco J. Varela, *The Tree of Knowledge: The Biological Roots of Human Understanding*, revised edition, trans. Robert Paolucci, (Boulder: Shambhala, 1998), 249.

In our darkest hours of realized loneliness, we run.

We turn to anything that can numb our reality.

The longer we fight it, the more we become subject to our numbing agents. We begin to withdraw from those closest to us, occasionally snapping at them when we exit the responsibility of connection and failing impact.

Avoidance becomes a tactic.

Relentless in our quest to be right, we are drama.

We claim roles of victimhood, rescue, and persecution, to be seen and to completely deflect our personal responsibility to be humane. We are cowards at best as we jockey for rank and recognition.

We begin to believe our own lies, including the one that "I am owed more than I am."

Ego at its finest.

Off putting.

We spend more time criticizing others than we ever spend looking for the good. Expressions of gratitude are so foreign to our existence, even though we would profess that we live in gratitude.

We operate from a place of fear. We try to control relevancy and in turn perpetuate more irrelevancy in the lives of those around us.

Welcome to the devil's dance. This is the place life will

begin to crumble underneath you—as if you didn't already feel it and know it, but you are too arrogant to accept it as something you hold sole responsibility for.

You've become entitled . . .

to nothing.

3 REFLECTIONS

In what areas of my life am I frustrated by others' lack of respect for who I am?

_____

_____

_____

_____

_____

Am I clean in my declarations, or am I living in hypocrisy?

_____

_____

_____

_____

Where am I avoiding the truth of who I am?

_____

_____

_____

_____

CRITICAL SKEPTICISM

"Beware the trappings of passionate dissatisfaction."

MOE

A few years back, I saw a T-shirt that had the words "THE CRITICAL SLIDE" written on it. Whether it meant what I took from it or not, it brought clearly to my own mind the slippery slope of criticism and aimed skepticism.

What I mean is simply this: your own bad attitude will never solve for someone else's incompetency.

While it's easy to find fault in another's actions (or lack thereof), it's far more difficult to identify one's own opportunity for change. That critical slide, as I've defined it here, leads nowhere. It's an empty path filled with anger and pent-up frustration that will continue to find a dead-end as it destroys every relationship in your life.

This chapter title contains two words that define a way of being toward others.

Each is both active and reactive.

When coupled together, these words can have a negative impact on our contribution and productivity.

For some, it's easier to avoid than to act. For others, it's far too easy to criticize openly in an attempt to assemble a diversionary army for personal avoidance.

At times, one can become soaked in the decay of criticism and overevaluation of others and self. Both are most often ego driven. Certainly the assertion of the right to cast a critical evaluation of another is a clear mark of someone expending effort in avoidance and procrastination of their own personal growth.

We build walls, fences, hidden passages, lonely corridors, and wasted rabbit holes when we engage in the craft of obstacle avoidance by focusing our time and attention on the criticism and non-belief in others. These structures and passages are so easily justified and inviting while also being rigid and defined by common dead-ends.

Criticisms that become justifications for stagnancy or a pass at growth serve neither us nor those we could be serving.

These easy walkways are typically founded in insecurity and fear, seeded in control and justification, and it's a trap.

When we spend too much time fixated on others, we lose sight of our own complex issues and our growth journey becomes stagnant.

Self-pity and constant complaining will always shut the door on creative inspiration.

When you find yourself in this trap, you'll begin to realize the fixation you've chosen has clouded your world and left you unable to focus.

Until you learn to de-haze this reactive cloud of insecurity, the conversations and focus that will occupy your days and nights will further delay all progress.

3 REFLECTIONS

How quick am I to assume, react, and then act based on a biased judgment?

_____

_____

_____

_____

_____

How often do I take a path of comfort rather than one that challenges my case?

_____

_____

_____

_____

_____

How ready am I to avoid the hard rather than embrace the right?

_____

_____

_____

_____

_____

DRAMA

"If every little annoyance is made into a great big drama, then a life of peace and greatness will forever elude you."[6]

BRENDON BURCHARD

---

[6]Brendon Burchard, Instagram (@brendenburchard), May 28, 2024 https://www.instagram.com/p/C7iA6RDKdOc/.

Living and acting in life's drama is one of the many ways we dance in a captive game.

When life is happening around us, we tend to want to claim some level of control with it or make meaning of the circumstances we experience along the way by claiming a "subject to" stance.

The great psychologist Stephen Karpman modeled and coined "The Drama Triangle"[7] as a prime example of manipulated interpretation and effort to CONTROL one's story and supporting framework for contention.

The model identifies a symbiotic relationship between three central characters that, when left untethered, can result in a destructive pattern among self and individuals contending with each other and the circumstances of their lives.

The three primary characters described in The Drama Triangle will be familiar to most of us. In fact, if you think of some of your favorite dramas from the big screen, you'll quickly realize that they each have central characters similarly described through Karpman's model.

In order for drama to exist and maintain itself, it must have all three characters in play. Those characters are the Victim, Rescuer, and Persecutor.

Each character has dependencies for identity maintenance, and all three must be present to stay in the drama

---

[7]Stephen Karpman proposed the social model of human interaction in 1968. "Karpman drama triangle," Wikipedia, https://en.wikipedia.org/wiki/Karpman_drama_triangle.

The Victim

In the Karpman Drama Triangle, the Victim feels helpless in their perceived setback. The concept of "life happening to them" is dominant. Their circumstances have been determined and shaped by someone other than themselves, and they are clear that someone or something is working against them, and there's nothing they can do to change it.

Many in this state will believe that their efforts are pointless. This paradigm gives them rest and a path of avoidance when facing real change. Life is complicated and unresolved when one is seeing life through this lens. Codependencies can develop with both the Persecutor and Rescuer, resulting in an ongoing state of drama.

The Rescuer

The Rescuer's motto is, "Let me help you." They feel guilty if they don't help and often become angry when their efforts fail. Rescuers keep Victims dependent on the Rescuer and their perceived support by colluding with the Victim in their victimhood.

By focusing on others, Rescuers avoid their own problems and feel good about helping, even though their main interest is being seen and acknowledged as helpful and in support of someone who is mired in oppression.

The Persecutor

The Persecutor does exactly that: they persecute others' stances or paradigms. They have a heavy interest in "being right" and someone else "being wrong." A Persecutor is often identified as a bully or someone without care or concern for another person's feelings or condition in life. Often dismissive, a Persecutor seeks to also build an army of supporters who believe the Persecutor's view of the Victim and even the Victim's Rescuer.

How Drama Starts

Drama starts when someone acts as a Victim or Persecutor and begins searching for others to justify their circumstance and position. This creates a natural conflict and battlefield. The first one to the party is usually the Rescuer, thus the triangle is complete, and the fun begins.

Dynamics and Motivations

Drama triangles continue because each person unconsciously has their needs met while they ignore the harm caused within the triangle. Each role serves selfish needs rather than genuinely helping the situation. The Rescuer's motivations are mixed: they seem to want to solve the problem but benefit from being seen as helpful and having someone depend on them.

Victims and Rescuers often have a codependent relationship, with the Rescuer keeping the Victim dependent on the Rescuer. People tend to have a habitual role they learned from their family, but once involved in a drama triangle, they can rotate through all three roles. Each role has a "payoff" that keeps the triangle going.

Interpersonal drama exists also as we seek to justify our ease and avoid our growth opportunities. We can become victims to our circumstance in life and we seek mental and emotional agreement within ourselves in the choice to delay rather than engage. Beliefs based on fixation of status or reduced hope can play out, and thus the harsh critic stares us down as our perpetual persecutor. Justification and "being right" become an easy game for the stuck.

The path of least resistance and victimhood is EASY.

It is weak in its foundation, and you'll find yourself on your butt more than your feet. The path of personal ownership, however, requires that we dismiss our ego, commit to the real even when it kicks us in the face, and pursue relentlessly an unwavering admission of personal ownership of the result.

It is EVERY DAY!

It's THE path to lasting results.

Avoid it, and it will find you again, and again, and again.

Are you ready to stop the madness?

3 REFLECTIONS

Where am I experiencing drama in my life?

_____

_____

_____

_____

_____

What character(s) am I playing in that drama?

_____

_____

_____

_____

Is it possible that I might play a bigger role in it than I thought?

_____

_____

_____

_____

REACTIVITY

"Action under stress often takes on the form of ill-founded reactivity."

MOE

Reactivity is often defined as an action taken in the moment. Quick to occur and often shortsighted, reactions tend to move us from pain or danger through a fight-or-flight response.

As an ever-evolving species, our brains are so magnificently designed to protect us and keep us alive through neural response to both stimulus and stored data.

In particular, we have a built-in neural filter referred to as the Reticular Activating System (RAS). Located in the brain stem is a network of neurons that project forward to the hypothalamus, backward to the thalamus, and directly to the cerebral cortex.

The RAS's primary role is focus, perception, and our fight-or-flight response to danger. It is a system of consciousness. As a justifier, it calls on previous experience and new programming to further reinforce what we deem necessary to identify and retain.

An example of this can be found in our everyday lives. Whether it be that new car we've had our eye on for the last several months or the repeated follies we find in a coworker, the brain is constantly processing what we feed it, holding onto what we deem most important or what we hold focus on.

As we condition it to see, feel, and watch for the programming, we quite literally design the filter to keep ONLY *those* things conscious, and stuff any other information into the dark cauldrons of the mind where they can have no impact on the present.

The red car we saw on the lot, the one we dreamed of and were certain would be limited in its existence, we now find everywhere on the roads the moment we drive off the lot.

The annoying coworker becomes more and more annoying, and everything about them now seems to further justify your belief in their intrusive existence.

In short, what you focus on becomes your reality. The RAS can be a tool for either progress or stagnant thinking ladened by bias and preconditioned attachment.

Now that we understand the brain a bit more, and particularly the RAS, I'd like to introduce you to a couple of self-coaching models—one designed by Brooke Castillo and the other designed by The Arbinger Institute.

The first model helps us better understand the inputs and connection between circumstance and action, and the end result.

The second model helps reinforce visually the dance between interpretation, action, receipt, and reaction. A vortex, when left unsolved, can result in utter destruction of relationship and opportunity.

CTFAR, Brooke Castillo

C: Circumstance (neutral)

T: Thoughts

F: Feelings

A: Actions

R: Results[8]

---

[8]Brooke Castillo, "The Model," found on The Life Coach School, https://thelifecoachschool.com/self-coaching-model-guide/.

The concept is that everything we might experience in our lives holds no value or meaning by the nature of pure circumstance until we decide to make something of it.

Circumstances are neutral as incidents undefined but factual in their definition. Examples of circumstance might be things like: the sky is blue; I stubbed my toe; there's dirt in the driveway; my tire is flat; someone drifted into my lane of traffic. All are circumstantial and facts of occurrence.

When one experiences a circumstance, the brain goes to work immediately to interpret the data. Thoughts about that thing come quickly, and there is often a conditioned response based on prior experience or adopted bias. Those thoughts emote a feeling and that feeling often leads to some form of action. Stack enough consistencies of thoughts, feelings, and actions, and you'll be able to predict and source your results.

Everything below the circumstance line is a chosen response and its associated result. While much of it might seem unconscious or quickly derived, we can choose our thoughts, feelings, and actions.

Let's take one of the circumstances I mentioned above: someone drifted into my lane of traffic.

When something like this occurs, quite often we formulate thoughts about that driver and their actions on the road. We might view them as reckless and rude. We might see them as irresponsible. We might decide they cut us off on purpose.

From those thought patterns, we quickly start to produce feelings. In this case, we might experience anger, frustration, fear, revenge, resentment, or rage.

The actions we take when we feel these things might include speeding up to show them they are "number one," honking the horn, shouting out loud an acknowledgment of their incompetence, attempting to pass them in rage, or whatever else suits our fancy and helps us feel better in that moment.

Eventually, the very thing we perceived about this driver and circumstance starts to become a more regular occurrence for us, and our level of road rage develops. And when the way we do one thing in life translates to the way we do everything, the next thing we know—our temper is shorter, our levels of patience and grace go out the window, and we're just plain spicy.

If we can control our thoughts, feelings, and subsequent actions, alternatives to the example above might be the thought and recognition that we, too, have inadvertently drifted into someone else's lane. It was accidental. The feelings we begin to have are grace and acceptance, followed by no action at all or a simple smile and wave to say it's okay.

Line enough of those new thoughts, feelings, and actions together and the results you'll realize in your life can be polar opposite.

THE CYCLE OF SELF DECEPTION, The Arbinger Institute[9]

Similar to the model above, what we experience and interpret can lead to actions that others then experience and interpret, resulting in their actions, which then lead to an evolved circumstance for us to observe, think on, and react to once again.

---

[9] The Arbinger Institute, *Leadership and Self-Deception: Getting Out of the Box*, 2nd edition (San Francisco: Beret-Koehler, 2010).

The model is illustrated below:

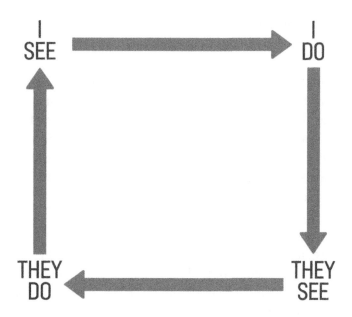

It's called a cycle for a reason. If left untamed, assumptions become the fuel, and misinterpretations and reactivity can produce unsavory results that destroy relationships and desired outcomes.

Once we are triggered, the brain moves fast to make meaning and protect our identity. Fight-or-flight becomes the reaction as we step on the stage for others to make meaning of our own actions.

I've always said that the space between stimulus and response is a gift. If you can find a way to honor this space before you act, you'll find hidden strength that was once masked by reactivity.

Awareness drives new opportunities.

Without a predetermined response and a plan of action for the choice that will come, we oftentimes find it impossible to keep up or even catch that choice point until it has come and gone.

It's then we realize that we had a choice, knew better, but refused to stop midpath to pause time and allow for an adjusted and more appropriate path forward.

This requires practice. It requires an awareness of self when triggered. It requires a daily commitment to start chipping away at Ego's persona.

One rule to stop the madness in both cases is to assume positive intent.

As mentioned earlier, CHOICE is one of our greatest gifts, and in this case, our choices lead to our realities.

Will you allow a pace and space for discovery and stillness, or will you avoid the change all together?

Your brain can be a useful tool if you'll start to recognize its usefulness beyond your normalcy.

We'll not find perfection here, but we will certainly be given ample practice time in this big game we call LIFE.

3 REFLECTIONS

Where have I made quick judgments in my life that have resulted in fast thinking and crummy results?

_____

_____

_____

_____

_____

In what ways can I SLOW DOWN my thinking to be less reactive and more aware of what is going on inside of my brain?

_____

_____

_____

_____

_____

Where can the practice of deliberate thoughts, feelings, and actions help me write a new story?

_____

_____

_____

_____

_____

JUDGMENT

"When you justify your own fears and doubts by repurposing them as an indifference toward others, the very thing you seek cannot be found."

MOE

Judgment comes quickly. It's cheap fuel built to protect the soul. Quite literally, it is our brain's sustaining mechanism to decide to fight change and quickly ascertain the truth we seek to substantiate our defined circumstance.

Biases and old patterns of absolution show up to the dance, blocking the way of new discovery.

Almost subconsciously, we enter protection mode when someone challenges our identity or preferred path.

We gather quickly contrived information—that may or may not be true—to dismantle our surrounding nemeses, avoiding a slower path of consideration and inquisition.

We make blanket assessments as absolutes without a possibility of future action.

We shut people out and paint an ill tinge on our perceived threats for others to see and hear.

Our actions and statements toward others or our circumstance are perfectly designed to once again reinforce our limiting bias toward the world around us.

Our threat has been avoided. Drama has maintained its pecking order. We have delayed the work of wonder.

One thing I've observed, unfortunately in both myself and others, is that selfish attempts to stoke your own ego will always result in low-level trust from those around you.

The simple truth is that when we seek to gain validation through self-serving tactics, we completely ignore the nature of our existence: to love, serve, and remember.

Our mind is clouded, closed, and hardened toward the opportunity to lift another and let go of the need to be right and be noticed.

Rumi reminds us: "Before you speak, let your words pass through three gates: Is it true? Is it necessary? Is it kind?"[10]

Judgment, when left unbridled, can take us down a path of shortsightedness and give us an inflated understanding of our own being.

When we consistently stack quick and passive judgments toward others, we limit our ability to see possibility and thus the path of progress continues to be marred and roadblocked by our inability to see and experience humanity.

Our impact on the world around us is short, weakened, and often limiting.

We experience an erosion of community and ultimately become the outcast due to our sloppy assumptions of others.

Alone, with no one left to judge but ourselves.

---

[10]Various sources attribute this to Rumi, though a specific work or correspondence is unverified (https://en.wikiquote.org/wiki/Rumi).

3 REFLECTIONS

How quick am I to assume, react, and then act against a person or circumstance based on a biased or quick judgment?

_____

_____

_____

_____

_____

How often do I take the path of comfort rather than one that challenges my case?

_____

_____

_____

_____

_____

How anxious am I to avoid the hard rather than embrace the right?

_____

_____

_____

_____

_____

CONTROL

"A frenetic pace is often a protective armor built to hide our cracks of vulnerability and control the world around us."

MOE

In a world with elements of unpredictability, we often try to control the uncontrollable and neglect those things we actually have a choice in. It's one of the gnarliest forms of being locked up and committed to a life of deceit and misery.

Examples of this are found in our desire to force our will on others in a need to be right, to be personally served, or to be hidden from the world.

In these self-serving moments and the grasp for control of our environment, we try to force an outcome and a choice on someone other than ourselves.

We remove our own responsibility to be in the moment as a contributor.

It's in these moments we seek to control that we force solidarity and ego, inciting drama and lack of cohesion. Alignment becomes a non-option as self-serving perception becomes the narrative.

Beware the pull and cloak of ease and its refrain.

It's a shortcut that will cut you short.

Control is a devil's game.

It's been that way from the beginning.

The degraded quest for certainty and subjected outcomes through overpowered paradigm and dominion is a failing attempt to win a game that has no place on the podium.

Ego is the sweet ingredient that fuels the need.

Justification, reactivity, false pretense, victimhood, avoidance, and fixation are the musty stench of the quest.

The chase and implied need to maintain a tight grip on a fractured and ungrounded reality in this world of imperfection can be gnawing and hollow.

When things are not going our way, we tend to want to alter or exert manipulated intent on the people in our lives to change our perceived circumstance and thus achieve a more desired output to align with our immediate need for safety, certainty, and maintained identity.

That was a long sentence, and one my editor will most likely want me to shorten. Nonetheless, it represents the chaotic narrative of control.

When we seek greater control in our lives, we take events of neutrality and work tirelessly to define their meaning without an opening for a shifted paradigm. We work to convince the world around us that our view of it, the story behind it, is not only justified but must remain true.

Placing expectations on our world and the players in it, we identify outcomes often unattainable or downright impossible given the frailty and myth of control.

Narcissistic behavior can often be found in the same camp, trying to control the people, places, and things of our world to alleviate our own pain and responsibility in the change we desire, in an effort to keep our own red-carpet party going.

We get stuck in our own traps. We grasp at things outside of our control, our grip so tight that our muscles fatigue and collapse around the objects of our lives.

Trying to control our own relevancy will create the opposite of what we want: less relevance rather than more.

Our leadership style is easily identified as "command and control." Our ability to inspire others is met with an empty room. "Trust," as a bartered concept, becomes an empty word, hollow in its expression as another arbitrated offering.

Our forced voice will leave us both empty and separated from a world we wished to define.

3 REFLECTIONS

How often am I trying to expedite someone else's opinion of me in order to predict a future outcome?

_____

_____

_____

_____

_____

What areas of my life are my expectations most often unmet?

_____

_____

_____

_____

How would someone describe my leadership style when I am under pressure?

_____

_____

_____

_____

_____

AT THE CROSSROAD

"As with most hard paths, you'll likely experience vistas never
imagined."

MOE

We've covered so much ground, yet, we have yet to begin.

It's certainly easy to observe and witness in others much of what has been covered already in this book. It's easy to see these behaviors and attributes in the characters of our world and raise our noses to such unbecoming behavior.

Self-awareness can be sketchy at times. In fact, at times it's nearly impossible, and thanks to a brilliantly designed brain, we have programmed that brain to avoid both the glaring truths and the dangers of change and surrender.

Do I see any of these behaviors when I look in the mirror?

Have others been sending me smoke signals all along that I do, indeed, have some unsightly characteristics that are causing further separation from a meaningful exchange with the world around me?

I often find myself in moments of exchange with fellow travelers, humans on the road of trial and inquisition. Beings developing. Their spoken and unspoken struggle with self and significance is beautiful. It brings with it an alert sense of being alive, and certainly finds people "in the arena."

One of my dear friends and personal mentors Katherine Eitel taught that "life is hard, until it's not." Confusing and flippant for some, this message only rings true and significant for those who have discovered this in its reality.

Hide and seek is the game of choice.

We hide.

We chase.

We wander from our best.

Lost, we start to find a being we know and love, who is familiar.

We start to experience an increased interest in the dissonance of this relationship.

Who do we see?

We see ourselves without the pain.

We see ourselves encompassed in light and connected to the real being who has yet to come forth and walk in the warmth of that light.

We experience the intimate crossroad of decision and risk.

Choice.

Choice to explore ourselves and our divinely appointed capacity for truth and humble significance.

We are faced with the incredible choice of letting go of our known and warm façade to take on a completely uncharted course into "the real."

The CHOICE, when faced head-on, will displace what you thought the arena was and place you squarely in the real arena of your life.

THIS is your holy place.

THIS is the place where God and His angels will march with you.

THIS is the place you will experience love and learn to love others.

THIS is the place where you experience LIVING TRUE.

May you be blessed in your personal and sacred journey into your truest state of creation and significance.

The place you were designed and appointed to.

It's your time.

Are you ready to start LIVING TRUE?

CHOICE

"Stewardship is the gateway between choice and freedom."

MOE

As with seasons of change, so, too, comes the realization that all cannot remain the same.

New growth comes only after a marked move from what once was.

As a natural course of progression, one must learn to let go of the past and lean into the future. It's that letting go that at times can feel so destructive and unsafe.

Stagnancy is easy and subconscious.

It's comfortable, until it becomes uncomfortable.

The mind-numb that begins to process as agitation and anxiousness becomes tangible.

Reality sets in that stagnancy has bred complacency and, ultimately, a misaligned death of the soul.

You wake up to find that the world around you is foreign and no longer feasible, and you find yourself on the battlefield facing two foes: suppression and avoidance.

I believe that the universe only holds reserved space for us in one of two areas: decision or indecision. However, it only rewards one with new providence.

If a new paradigm exists as a choice, then how might adopting a paradigm that new growth will require the destruction of a misaligned past serve your future self?

In order to make room for certainty, you must be willing to let go of uncertainty.

If we want the bright horizon of tomorrow to be different from the familiar and dim glow of today, we must be willing to loosen the grip we have on our fixation of the past.

We must be willing to lay down our old, comfortable self so we can redefine and move toward our future best self.

I believe the greatest gift in our mortal lives is the gift of choice. How we honor that gift will shape the eternities.

CHOICE is the grandest gift in our lives and subsequently one of our greatest superpowers.

It is so powerful and tied directly to our mortal journey that even God Himself would cease to exist if He took it away.

It's ours to explore and work with. It holds us armed with options in any given circumstance.

Given that . . . YOU HAVE THIS MOMENT to choose your path forward and to intentionally act on behalf of your being.

This fantastic question from my dear friend and mentor Alan Ayers perhaps sums it up:

HOW DO YOU WANT TO FEEL?

ENTER the CROSSROAD.

The crossroad has two distinct choices:

1. Remain unchanged, chained to a life of duality and empty chase, getting further away from a life of significance and meaningful impact and closer to one that leaves you lonely and broken.

2. Change course by taking a NEW path that will certainly challenge you, one that will set you free. A road of meaning and connection.

As one of my mentors Jeff Wilmore once said, "living true is expensive."

Expensive, in that it will test relationships. It will beg you to make clear and concise decisions that vary from a habituated past. It will test you as a parent, spouse, friend, colleague, leader. And it will test you in your weakest moments. You'll toil with walking away from the busy by narrowing your focus on what matters most. It might find you facing displacement from work and community. However, this road holds the promise of the real and unhidden. It's here where you will feel most loved and offer the most to those on similar journeys of leaving behind an unfruitful and disconnected existence.

REMAIN LOCKED—or—TURN THE KEY.

If you choose option 1 (REMAIN LOCKED):

You can close the book here and continue as you have been, armed with new information but committed to the safety of dissonance for now. I am grateful for you and your personal journey. I lived many years in this place and know it quite well. I wish you the very best and want to thank you personally for picking up the book and investing your time and interest in it.

If you choose option 2 (TURN THE KEY):

Slow down. Breathe in. Feel your heart beating. Arm yourself with the deep love and commitment you hold for those you are fighting for. Envision yourself on the other side of this grand leap standing tall, LIVING TRUE to who you were divinely appointed to become.

Let go of the safety and familiarity of your past.

Make the leap.

Turn the page.

You'll now be reading the UNLOCKED version, which represents a life being lived in and how it might begin to look and feel as you live true.

Enjoy your journey, my friend. I honor you in this noble pursuit and pray that you will feel a beautiful lift and recognize providence as it meets you on this special road.

It's time!

HUMILITY

"On the battlefield of personal change, ego must learn to surrender to humility."

MOE

What does it feel and look like to be humble? As I have reflected over the years about attributes and actions, when it comes to "humility," I've found the following statements or descriptions to be true:

Freedom from pride and arrogance

Open

Teachable

Meek

Having a childlike wonderment

One who doesn't take things personally while taking true ownership for their own mistakes

Freedom from the need to be right—without a rush to criticize others

Open to the possibility of change

Everpresent to one's own responsibilities

Full of grace and love toward another and their journey

Quiet

Not boastful

Comfortable and confident in one's own unique skin

Aware of how one shows up in the world, with a sensitivity to impact and influence through example

More doing and less talking

Without the constant need to prove worth or value

Operating from a place of service

Patient with the journey

Patient with social interaction

Not reactive or spun up by someone else's reactivity

Bold, but not brash

Actively allowing space for someone else to shine

Willing to take the blame when things go wrong, and openly celebrating others when things go right

Reduced levels of control and arrogance

Having a keen sense of enough

I remember, from my youth, watching my own father display a way of being toward others and circumstance. One of the phrases I often heard him quote was "what shall it profit a man to be right if he thereby makes an enemy?" He was not easily ruffled by drama and, more often than not, he was the constant champion for others when they were not in the room. He was patient and kind. He was and is a tangible example to me of what humility means. I reflect upon his example often and realize that humility coupled with grace is a foundational ingredient for a life well lived and one of meaningful impact.

Humility is a cornerstone of selflessness.

Humility is the ability to see yourself in the context of a much bigger world.

One of my all-time favorite quotes on feedback and criticism is this:

"Don't mind criticism. If it is untrue, disregard it. If it is unfair, keep from irritation. If it is ignorant, smile. If it is justified, learn from it."

I've not been able to source where it came from or who said it, nonetheless, it has become one of the most useful reminders to both me and many I have served along the road of what a humble approach to criticism might look like.

From the Bible we have the example of Christ and His ministry. He served. He sacrificed personal comfort and recognition for the success and progress of others. He didn't complain or draw attention to himself for cause, rescue, or rapport. He knew His mission and was resolute in His efforts to be and become a noble and honored Son of God through obedience and diligence. He was without guile, free of deceit and hypocrisy. He was found consistent by both his followers and his enemies. He understood clearly the cost of living true and did it anyway. His humility was found in His loving service to each of us.

When it comes to humility, "others first" becomes the motto.

When you live this way, the complexities of needing to be right and in control of your reference point in the world goes away.

People naturally engage with you.

They want to dance because they feel there is a space to do so confidently and without criticism for their lack.

You are not in the way but rather a welcome partner.

3 ACTION STEPS

1. Make a habit of taking a moment at the end of each day to reflect on all the people who were part of making you successful on that day. This helps you develop a natural sense of humility, allowing you to see how you are not the only cause of your success. End the reflection by actively sending a message of gratitude to those people.

2. In your own quiet place of reflection, consider where you are active in wanting to be seen, heard, and in control of your world. Ask yourself why that is and whom it might be serving. Develop an action plan to create new habits that can help you give space for others and curb your need to be the central figure in your association with others.

3. Start to pay attention to the varying levels of humility in those around you. Sometimes, through others' examples and ways of being, we can be inspired and led to new choices and a kinder way of being.

GRATITUDE

"Gratitude turns what we have into enough, and more. It turns denial into acceptance, chaos into order, confusion into clarity . . . it makes sense of our past, brings peace for today, and creates a vision for tomorrow."[11]

MELODY BEATTIE

---

[11]Melody Beattie, *The Language of Letting Go: Daily Meditations on Codependency*, (Center City: Hazelden, 1990), 218.

I recall a moment when I was a teenager that I started to feel the weight of obligation, responsibility, and perhaps a bit of overwhelm to go with it. One day, I was working in the family business and was being pulled in numerous directions. It was busy and at the peak of the customer season. It seemed that every spare moment I had to catch a breath was quickly filled with another task of high urgency. No matter what I did, it seemed I couldn't keep up.

I can see clearly the moment I reached for the door to attend to a customer request in the parking lot when I looked back at my mother, with tears welling up in my eyes. She knew of my struggle at that moment. With a smile on her face, she said, "Slow down, Art. You just need to learn to laugh a little and smile. It's all going to be okay. Even when life seems hard, if you will learn to laugh at it and smile, life will get a lot easier."

I will always remember that moment.

In fact, I believe that moment was one of many installations in my personal journey to see life as being filled with joy and possibility rather than feeling as though life was a miserable extended sentence to be lived in.

One of my favorite poems is one by Sara Teasdale, titled "Barter."

Life has loveliness to sell,
   All beautiful and splendid things,
Blue waves whitened on a cliff,
   Soaring fire that sways and sings,
And children's faces looking up
Holding wonder like a cup.

Life has loveliness to sell,
   Music like a curve of gold,
Scent of pine trees in the rain,
   Eyes that love you, arms that hold,
And for your spirit's still delight,
Holy thoughts that star the night.

Spend all you have for loveliness,
   Buy it and never count the cost;
For one white singing hour of peace
   Count many a year of strife well lost,
And for a breath of ecstasy
Give all you have been, or could be.[12]

---

[12]Sara Teasdale, "Barter," in *Love Songs*, (New York: Macmillan, 1918), 3.

In short, I believe that we are surrounded by incredible vistas and moments that are so easy to pass by and ignore if we are not willing to take the time to notice and savor them.

We have much to be grateful for. One of the greatest gifts we possess is the gift of choice.

With this powerful gift we can choose to look, listen, and feel, or we can simply choose to ignore the world around us.

Some moments we might choose to see and absorb, holding internal what moved us.

Some moments we might experience and freely express the wonder as an invitation for others to feel so too.

Regardless of our walk on this beautiful planet, if we are to experience joy, we must learn to be an active participant and architect in that quest. It requires daily practice. It requires that we slow down enough to truly experience the world around us. It requires that we actively reflect on and welcome the noticeable gratuities of each day.

I have a theory about sunsets and people. Some people will stop what they are doing to acknowledge and savor a sunset while others will simply be unaware or actively ignore it as a distraction. I believe the happier of the two are those that seek and spend time with one of God's daily gifts to us.

One more thought on what we experience in our lives.

When something resonates and finds meaning within us, it is for us to use in that moment, but it is also a gift for us to give away so that someone else might be given the opportunity to benefit from it.

Be patient while the music breathes.

It's the music between the notes that helps us see and hear.

3 ACTION STEPS

1. Pay attention to the little things in life.

2. Look for the good in others.

3. Let them know.

ACCEPTANCE

"Don't mind criticism. If it is untrue, disregard it. If it is unfair, keep from irritation. If it is ignorant, smile. If it is justified, learn from it."

ANONYMOUS

I distinctly recall one evening as I was lying in bed next to my sweetheart, a conversation that would spark deep inquisition and become the catalyst for much-needed change.

In a quiet and kind way she turned to me and said,

"You are not the man I married. You have hardened. Our children are afraid to engage with you, and I no longer feel like I'm your number one."

Wow! I couldn't believe what I was hearing. I remember asking some questions in an attempt to litigate this expressed reality, while simultaneously feeling a nudge to stop talking, listen, and in a mature and loving way internalize the feedback I had just received.

To say I was confused would be an understatement. I remember this time in my life like it was yesterday. I was on full tilt, doing everything I could to become a better man, or so I thought. I was engaged in personal development. I felt like I was more aware of the people in my life and my way of being in the world. I felt like I was trying to engage with my children more and I knew intimately my prayer each night to better honor the two great stewardships of my life: those of husband and father.

How could the person that I loved the most, someone I craved for her companionship each waking moment, not see my efforts or feel my love?

From the Grateful Dead's "Scarlet Begonias" Robert Hunter's lyrics rang true:

"Once in a while you get shown the light
In the strangest of places if you look at it right."[13]

I was rocked to the core. If what I was hearing was true, where would I even begin to change how those I loved the most experienced me?

Was what I'd just heard and experienced important enough to internalize it and get to work creating the necessary changes to shift an eroding world around me?

YES! Without question!

This incredible woman had just shared with me something I'm sure was difficult for her and was a reality that had hit a fever pitch in her own life and in the lives of those she, too, cared deeply for.

As I started to break down what I had heard into manageable components, it started to become clearer to me how I had become habituated to my own life and way of being with others.

When it came to my children, I was short with them, distracted, and not present most of the time. I saw their gaps more than I saw their gains. I was regularly absent from the home, working to provide a more robust lifestyle, while abandoning the very thing they treasured more than anything: time.

When it came to my spouse, I was distracted by a phone that was attached to my hip and rang at all hours of the day and night, which I justified as a necessity to my role and efforts to provide for her and our children. I was giving tremendous effort and time to a job, becoming fully absorbed and

---

[13]"Scarlet Begonias" lyrics by Robert Hunter, music composed by Jerry Garcia, recorded by The Grateful Dead in 1974, released June 27, 1974 on *From the Mars Hotel*, CBS Studios.

entrenched in creating something that felt helpful and noble.

The problem with this is that it left very little time for real presence in the home. They got my table scraps at best.

I had become nothing more than a passing freight train.

The biggest issue I was beginning to see was that I had stopped listening to others' opinions and started to justify my way of being, and the behavior of those around me, as necessary and right. I had started to adopt the attitudes and paradigms of those whom I was spending the most time with.

My whole world had been shaped by an immersion in the thick of thin things.

I had become the product of the people I spent the most time with. I was transfigured by my tribe, and not in a good way.

I had allowed myself to become something that was the polar opposite of what I truly wanted to be—an incredible father to our children—and for my sweetheart to know and feel without question that she was my number one.

I had work to do.

I knew I needed to wake up and shake off my habituated state.

I had to get far more intentional and present to the real stuff that mattered to me and my loved ones.

I had to start identifying boundaries and, more importantly, begin to build and create a life of meaning with them.

I remain ever grateful for this time in my life when I was

afforded love and candor from those who mattered most.

My ongoing efforts are and will continue to be focused on becoming the man I know I can become for the people in my life who count on me the most.

One of my all-time favorite quotes is found in the header of this chapter. I am reminded by it often that if we remain open to feedback and criticism, there are times we might find some of our greatest treasures therein.

In his book titled *Relationomics*, Dr. Randy Ross refers to "The Poor Man's 360,"[14] a single question intended to provide the one asking it the raw unfiltered feedback they so desperately need to hear. If set up the right way, we should be asking for the hard-to-say things from those in our relational casting. Most people will give us about 50% of what they want to say because they fear our reaction or retribution. This holdback doesn't serve either party. Resentment and distancing continue when left unaddressed.

Ask for it all when you ask this single, profound question:

"What's it like being on the other side of me?"

Give the responder the time and space, and more importantly the respect, to truly listen to what they have to say.

WARNING: do not ask this question if you aren't ready to humbly hear and act on the answer.

I have learned to use The Poor Man's 360 more frequently in my efforts to become a better spouse, father, friend, and leader.

---

[14]Dr. Randy Ross, *Relationomics: Business Powered by Relationships*, (Ada: Baker, 2019).

This type of feedback has the power to transform your life if you will allow yourself to let go of your ego and to step into the unknown of becoming better for the world around you.

3 ACTION STEPS

1. With those who matter most to you, effectively set up and establish the trust necessary to engage The Poor Man's 360.

2. When you are receiving feedback, kindly listen and internalize without debate or retribution.

3. Courageously map your course correction and give it your highest attention.

CREATION

"Creation as an attribute is a divine inheritance."

MOE

Before being sent to this earth, each one of us was intentionally and divinely designed by a Creator who knew us and built us in His likeness.

Because of this, we have internal seeds of impact and contribution.

Quite literally, we were built to build!

Creation necessitates the abandonment of excuses and finger-pointing by requiring that you take full ownership of the outcomes you seek in your life.

In this chapter's counterpart, titled" DRAMA," we learned about The Karpman Triangle and the central characters of it. We learned about the dependency that exists between characters and the fuel that perpetuates it in our lives.

In one of the most masterful counterworks to drama, David Emerald developed a model he identified as "The Empowerment Dynamic." In fact, he wrote a fantastic book about it that's become one of my favorites: *The Power of TED.*

In his model Emerald identified three opposing, or counter characters, to Karpman's Drama Triangle.

Emerald's model is all about the go-forward.

The alternative character to a Victim is a Creator.

The alternative character to a Persecutor is a Challenger.

The alternative character to a Rescuer is a Coach.

The Creator

A Creator might ask questions of themself with the intention of finding opportunity and new paths forward. Questions like, "Given the situation, how might I make the most of it?" or "What is mine to own here?"

A Creator will approach perceived setbacks with eyes wide open, with a sense of humility and ownership for the best next move forward.

The Challenger

A Challenger lets go of the need to be right and focuses instead on growth and learning for those they are in contact with, even in spite of perceived difficulties and potential drama.

A Challenger might ask questions like, "What other possibilities might be true, given the circumstance?" or "Where can we stay consistent with our values and still move forward?"

A Challenger sees people for where they are at and acknowledges the circumstance, all while providing an alternative paradigm or productive path forward.

Simon Sinek speaks of being the type of leader that others will follow. Leaders of high impact and influence naturally know those they serve and will challenge from a place of competence and consideration for the path of those they are in life with.

In building on Simon's notion of leadership, I would say this: be the type of leader that others will gladly follow, so that when you take them into their dangerous place they will feel safe.

The Coach

A Coach partners with the other person by asking better questions—questions designed to give the power of choice and deeper thinking a chance at finding a constructive path forward.

Great Coaches understand ownership of outcome and an individual's direct responsibility for their own journey. In moments of perceived setback, a Coach also refrains from doing something for someone that person can do for themself.

A Coach might ask questions like, "If you had even more courage than you do now, what would you do next?" or "What are you most clear about?"

The two models you are now becoming more acquainted with are worlds apart. One is limited through oppression and stagnancy (Drama), while the other is rooted in creation and ownership (Empowerment).

Creation is a choice and is requisite for further progression. Creation in its essence is a decision to build from the ashes.

There will be obstacles.

People will let you down.

You will be served all sorts of tasty distractions in the forms of setbacks and opposition.

You'll lose your way. You'll find your way.

Those who acknowledge this, own it, and choose to rise anyway will find consistently better results in their lives.

This new road is a place where:

1. Obstacles are repurposed and invited as necessary stepping stones.

2. Letdowns become a non-issue as you learn to lead rather than please.

3. Distractions, when recognized for what they are, will cease to draw you in.

4. The unknown becomes the desired path and thus, the way.

5. Every defeat becomes a clear invitation to own the next round.

One thing you might consider is praying for the insight and wisdom to learn about your divine identity. You have unique gifts and talents you've been blessed with.

Your life is meant for more and providence will be on your side as you own your existence and the possibility of true impact and influence.

3 ACTION STEPS

1. Identify the areas in your life where you can shift from a character in drama to a more powerful version of yourself as either a Creator, Challenger, or Coach.

2. Map out the opportunities to be found in your perceived setbacks. They are there, but you have to SLOW DOWN enough to look for them.

3. Go make something. Create from a place of calling and service to humanity. Do the thing that you are resisting.

SLOW DOWN

"It's the music between the notes that helps us see and hear."

MOE

Dieter F. Uchtdorf explained that,

> patience is not passive resignation, nor is it failing to act because of our fears. Patience means active waiting and enduring. It means staying with something and doing all that we can—working, hoping, and exercising faith; bearing hardship with fortitude, even when the desires of our hearts are delayed. patience is not simply enduring; it is enduring well!
>
> Impatience, on the other hand, is a symptom of selfishness. It is a trait of the self-absorbed. It arises from the all-too-prevalent condition called "center of the universe" syndrome, which leads people to believe that the world revolves around them and that all others are just supporting cast in the grand theater of mortality in which only they have the starring role.[15]

---

[15] Dieter F. Uchtdorf, "Continue in Patience," talk at the 180th Semi-Annual General Conference of The Church of Jesus Christ of Latter-day Saints, Conference Center in Salt Lake City, Utah, April 3, 2010.

In my own life experience, I've come to realize that it's the music between the notes that helps us see and hear.

What that means is that there's brilliant learning and advice that always comes during moments of chaos and unrest if we will just SLOW DOWN and be fully present in the moment, rather than hurrying for the time to pass.

There's wisdom available if we will set down the phone, turn off the TV, get to higher ground, and just listen.

What you'll see, feel, and hear will be the lesson meant for you in that very moment.

The brain moves quickly. Our windows of thinking are governed by the time and conditions we allow for their expanse.

There's a marked difference between fast and slow thinking.

We live in a world that is outpacing our ability to adapt as a human race.

Neural pathways are shrinking.

Our ability to obtain and meaningfully consume information is battling an instantaneous swipe and quick move to the next thing.

Digital dementia is on the rise while AI technology is replacing creativity.

Relationships with self and others are collapsing under the guise of "busy."

For those seeking to be more efficient and effective, there are two mantras that challenge pace:

slow down to speed up,

and

take the time it takes so that it takes less time.

Some of the greatest lessons and opportunities in my life have come during moments of elected slowdown.

Be patient while the music breathes.

As a test, read through the following poem.

COURAGE IS CALLING

Fear of the dark.
Holdback.
Questions . . .
Light trickling from an unacquainted horizon.
The resistance.
Friends. Foes. Philanthropy.
Creations conundrum.
Calling. Purpose. Passion. Trade . . .
Time.
Equations.
Past.
A heartbeat. Beat. Beating.
Courage is calling.
Dark acquaintance.
History told.
Proliferation . . .
A dance with faith tested.
Gnawing at the bone.
Tired.
The light of a new dawn.
The promise of the road.
The whirlwind of a reckoning.
Bold. Beautiful. Brave.
Void. Insoluble. Heroic . . .
Who? How? When?
Commitment. Duty. A tear . . .
Alive. Polarized. Quiet.
Truth. Telling. Rest.
Now?
Courage is calling.

Now, I challenge you to go back and reread this poem.

SLOW DOWN.

Every word and piece of punctuation was chosen to help you feel the message. Find yourself in it.

There will always be music between the notes if you'll allow yourself to spend time with life and actually live in it.

3 ACTION STEPS

1. Take a walk in nature without distraction (no phone, music, or book playing in the background) and by yourself. Look. Listen. Feel. Walk slower than you normally would. Breathe. Notice. Then journal your experience.

2. SLOW DOWN enough to see the blank page in front of you.

3. Intentionally design and follow through on a media or tech fast of your own. Journal what you observe.

CURIOSITY

"Be curious, not judgmental."[16]

JASON SUDEIKIS as TED LASSO

---

[16] *Ted Lasso*, season 1, episode 8, "The Diamond Dogs," directed by Declan Lowney, written by Jason Sudeikis, Bill Lawrence, and Brendan Hunt, starring Jason Sudeikis, Hannah Waddingham, and Jeremy Swift, aired September 18, 2020, Apple TV.

If we want bigger results in our lives, we must learn to ask bigger questions of ourselves. Questions have the power to move us from stagnancy into action. How often are we in inquisition, seeking to understand rather than working to be seen?

Consideration is synonymous with curiosity. When we are open to others' perspectives, we allow for our own pre-determinations to potentially be challenged.

A habit to be aware of is making blanket statements and absolutions about someone based on recent or past experience.

An example of this might be an assertion that "so-and-so can't be trusted." This blanket assessment leaves no possibility for future action and thus leaves an impression of fixation relative to the person of interest.

When we learn to ground assessments such as this, we start to ask questions meant to find opportunities for future action and we learn to clarify the context of the original casting.

If the absolution is that "so-and-so can't be trusted," I might ask if that is in every domain of their life or somewhere specific. I might choose to inquire more about where that person has demonstrated being trustworthy. Can they be counted on to go to bed when they are tired? Do they show up on time for work? Are they a law-abiding citizen?

You get the idea.

Curiosity takes us into a space of discovery and possibility.

One of the coolest questions I've heard is this:

What do I know to be true that isn't?

This question challenges the very premise that we might have a paradigm that could be challenged or that might not be entirely accurate. It exposes the possibility that we might have subconscious fixations and biases.

When we learn to operate from a place of curiosity, we let go of the need to control voice and interpretation.

We allow space for the new and we learn to govern our shallowness.

3 ACTION STEPS

1. Identify areas of your life you might be making blanket and ungrounded assessments.

2. Ask yourself this question: What would I need to know about the people in my life so I can delay my immediate and reactive judgment of them?

3. Find someone you've never spoken with and ask them for 15 minutes of their time. Your job is to ask them questions. The deeper the questions, the more you'll get to know them. Do your best to let them fill the space by being slow to interrupt or move onto the next question. Afterward, acknowledge anything that might have stood out to you. Thank them for their time, and let them get back to their day. Journal what you learned.

LETTING GO

"In this world where the land has mostly been explored, our personal explorations take place in the heart and mind. This is a journey of uncharted waters for most of us, an adventure both treacherous and exhilarating. Treacherous in that we must let go of the security of false or partial truth. Exhilarating because we move to a new realm of performance, a zone seldom achieved by the status quo."[17]

DAVID COOK

---

[17]David Cook, *Golf's Sacred Journey, the Sequel: Seven More Days in Utopia*, (Grand Rapids: Zondervan, 2018), 40.

As I settle in with my own personal thoughts and feelings, I am experiencing the dichotomy of letting go. My life has been a whirlwind over the last 48 hours. My mind and body have been called into a state of anxious deliberation.

For the last 11 years I have been actively engaged as an executive for a beautiful company. This season of service has represented nearly half of my career. The gratitude I feel for the personal growth I have experienced runs deep, as it has certainly helped shape some of my identity. The people have been choice, the ground we've walked together sacred.

And then this . . .

It's complete.

It's time to let go.

I'm moving on and into the unknown.

The choice to enter a new season.

It feels raw and unsafe, and I have no doubt it will come with failures and setbacks.

It will challenge my identity.

My season is changing.

The dichotomy in the promise of change:

　Increased strength

　Increased wisdom

　Increased grace

THIS is the real of the forward! A road unexplored and unexperienced, and part and parcel with our mortal journey to explore the edges of our comfort.

Whenever I have a client that is anxious for greener pastures, I ask them this question:

Are you running from something, or running to something?

Like all good questions, it certainly causes a moment of pause and reflection for what is really going on.

For some, it's a clear attempt to flee the scene.

For others, it's an eager and excited leaning into the creative frontier of the new.

More often than not, it's the combo platter. Something about the gnaw of dissonance and draw of one's truth just seems to be the call of seasons shifting.

In one of the closing scenes of Ted Lasso, Coach Beard, Ted's longtime assistant and friend, is having difficulty letting go of his solidified belief around Nate's betrayal of the team. It's a feeling and story he's held onto tightly out of a sense of loyalty to and defense of AFC Richmond and those on the pitch.

Ted recognizes the stranglehold it's having on Coach Beard, and in a moment of clarity and kindness he leans into his role as a trusted mentor and friend. Ted reminds Coach Beard, in vivid detail, of the road the coach once traveled and what extended grace on his behalf meant for him then and now. As the conversation between the two comes to a close, Ted shares this profound statement:

"I hope that either all of us or none of us are judged by the actions we take in our weakest moments, but rather for the strength we show if and when we're given a second chance."[18]

I couldn't help but think of the many second chances that had been offered on my own behalf. I knew the struggle Coach Beard was experiencing in the grip of pride and "be right." However, in this moment, I understood grace even more than I thought I had.

The "Serenity Prayer" offers this reprise:

"God, grant me the serenity to accept the things I cannot change, the courage to change the things I can, and the wisdom to know the difference."

It's a clear and present reminder of what lies in our hands and what doesn't while also representing a plea for the peace and serenity that lies on the other side of control. It's a prayer for new habit.

Life is in motion.

The earth we stand on is revolving with certainty, but it does not revolve around us.

Life whirls by us at a pace we don't control, nor should we try. However, in the spin we have moments of pause and clarity and personal opportunity.

In those rendered moments, take careful note of the promptings to serve another. Look for the inclinations to

---

[18] *Ted Lasso*, season 3, episode 11, "Mom City," directed by Declan Lowney, written by Jason Sudeikis, Bill Lawrence, and Brendan Hunt, starring Jason Sudeikis, Hannah Waddingham, and Jeremy Swift, aired May 24, 2023, Apple TV.

show up better. Be careful not to ignore the wisdom that flows when you learn to listen and act on those things that promote growth.

Life starts easy and ends easy if we learn to navigate the middle. It's that middle that trips us up a bit. We see, compare, devise, act out, run from, embrace, fold, criticize . . . the list could go on and on. When we wake up and listen to the lesson available to us telling us to let go—let go of the need to control—and hold tight to the prospect of growth that can only be funded through personal responsibility; and share the lessons; and serve one another; and put in the work . . .

When we do this, the spin and spoil of life no longer claims our horizon but rather allows us to SEE a new path. A path lined with clarity and an acknowledgment of the simple truth that comfortable won't serve you. It never has and it never will.

It's in letting go that we realize creation and destruction can dance in a similar paradigm.

As with seasons of change, so too comes the realization that all cannot remain the same. New growth comes only after a marked move from what once was. In a natural course of progression, one must learn to let go of the past and lean into the future. It's that letting go that at times can feel so destructive and unsafe.

I believe that the universe only holds reserved space for us in one of two areas: decision or indecision. However, it only rewards one area with new providence.

If a new paradigm exists as a choice, then how might adopting a paradigm that new growth will require the destruction of a misaligned past serve your future self?

In order to make room for certainty, you must be willing to let go of uncertainty.

If we want the bright horizon of tomorrow to be different from the familiar and dim glow of today, we must be willing to loosen the grip we have on our fixation of the past.

We must be willing to lay down our old, comfortable self to redefine and move toward our future best self.

If you're itching for a change but having trouble letting go of the habits creating your present existence, dive into the reality of change as a chosen paradigm.

It's your time!

Life was built for us and to challenge us in our imperfect way of being. The opportunities in front of us are just that: they are in the here and now of today's choice.

We have this moment.

Are you ready to explore the you that God built you to be?

Are you ready to unlock the gifts and existence that have been endowed in you?

3 ACTION STEPS

1. Identify where you've got a tight grip on life and fixed being.

2. Ask God for help to understand and let go of those fixations (the "Serenity Prayer").

3. Make the choice and move forward in faith that all will be well or as it should be, even in its imperfection.

THE AWAKENING

"When life gets blurry, get to higher ground."

MOE

I found myself so disoriented, wandering, and afraid of what I saw in the mirror.

I was frightened by the realization that my past and present missteps were outpacing my future.

I was lost and I didn't even realize it.

I had no idea how far off the path I had wandered, yet on the other hand, I was allowing life to unfold in an alarming way.

I was aimlessly trying to justify an easy road out.

Life was blurry.

For those of you who are reading this book, I want to remind you that it was written for you.

What I felt is not uncommon. It's easy to get caught up in the messiness of life and our active play in it. When we experience a raw level of dissonance in our lives, we inherently crave some form of relief. Unfortunately, we often seek relief in more of the same unbecoming behavior by choosing paths that lead us further from our truest self. The dopamine chase allows short bursts of temporary distraction from living a courageous life.

These seasons of life are messy.

They are chaotically slow.

These are seasons when we openly battle the being we want to bring forth.

ADVICE:

WHEN LIFE GETS BLURRY, GET TO HIGHER GROUND.

There's a place I have felt drawn to over the years, over and over again. I have found solace and recharge there.

A place where my soul is challenged and embraced by a loving God.

Higher ground.

Ever since I can recall, I have always been drawn to the mountains. I remember from my youth countless opportunities I had to be outdoors, whether it was camping, exploring, or playing. The mountains have always been a place that gives me lift.

I've spent time climbing cliff walls and navigating wild rivers. I've backpacked into remote lakes and slept under the stars.

What is it about these places or experiences, though, that fill my cup?

Come with me.

Let's go there.

For it is in the quiet that you will receive what you need.

When life gets blurry, get to higher ground.

When you are there just look, listen, and feel . . .

Take it all in.

You'll find that there is a lesson for you.

The wild is where God paints.

Go beyond where the road ends.

Sit with His presence and observe the magnitude of His love and creation all around you.

Slow down.

Breathe.

Let go.

In His creation you will see your unique and significant part in a grander design. You will feel a new respect for the world around you. You will sense the magnitude of a world much bigger and more full of grace than you hold for it.

Love is the feeling and clarity the gift.

I've never heard these lyrics like I hear them now:

"You can't start a fire
Worryin' about your little world fallin' apart."[19]

Letting go requires great courage and faith in a future undefined and waiting for you.

There is love available for you.

---

[19]"Dancing in the Dark," written and performed by Bruce Springsteen, recorded February 14, 1984 at The Hit Factory, single released March 8, 1984, Columbia, 12-inch vinyl.

Let's go there together.

Higher ground has become my favorite place.

I hope it will become yours.

CONCLUSION

"The reward of growth that comes through sacrifice is a precious gift that strengthens our value of choice and its eternal consequence."

MOE

This story started between the towns of Eden and Liberty, Utah.

Beautiful and majestic.

A place where I experienced my deepest fears and envisioned my greatest joys. A place where choice became a priority, and I committed myself to a path into the unknown. A decision meant for living true to the promises I had made both mortally and pre-mortally was all I had.

It was a place of raw acquaintance with what mattered most.

Perhaps that's symbolic of where our mortal ancestry began as well—in a garden called Eden, pure and unfettered by the failings of this mortal existence—a place where the physical had yet to be determined.

In both cases, sin and redemption were found by and through the grace of God.

On the other side of redemption, one finds freedom.

Freedom from the complexities of duality and subconscious living. Freedom from the haze of greed and ego.

Freedom to become that which our Creator designed us to be.

Perhaps the grandest question of them all is this:

HOW DO YOU WANT TO FEEL?

You see, there are layers, so there will be more for another day, another verse, another story, all along this road we've been given.

I hope that you'll recognize the greatest gift in your life to be the gift of choice.

I hope you'll take great care to honor that gift.

The promise of LIVING TRUE is eternal in its reward.

I honor your unique journey and the choices you will face along the way.

And should our paths cross one another, I hope that you'll slow down to say hello, and perhaps take in a sunset next to me, my friend.

"Life has loveliness to sell . . . buy it and never count the cost."[20] —Sara Teasdale

---

[20]Sara Teasdale, "Barter," in *Love Songs*, (New York: Macmillan, 1918).

ACKNOWLEDGMENTS

Writing this book has been a labor of love.

It would not have been possible without the constancy of love and support from my dear Melanie. She has been, and continues to be, the being that helps me transcend my fears and doubts.

To my children, Chyllia, Kensley, and Rylyn, you continue to provide me the gift of opportunity to be a better father and to live true each day to the promise of responsibility.

To my friends whom I am fortunate to experience life with, your input and support mean the world to me.

Of particular note, I'd like to thank my good brother Alan Ayers, a modern-day lyricist who will one day be welcomed by the Great Gig in the Sky as their missing band member. His love of language and uncovered meaning is remarkable, and his friendship leaves nothing unturned.

To my clients and colleagues, you've been on this road with me. Your trust in me leaves me honored and committed to doing my best each day and, perhaps more importantly, committed to sharing the gift and lessons learned of and experienced along the way. (Alan, mentioned above, along with my friend and colleague Noall Knighton, taught me one of the great standards of leadership regarding passing along knowledge and experience: "Watch one. Do one. Teach one.") This book is just that, a passing of the baton.

To my editor, Mindy Peterman, thank you for your patience and expertise. Your assistance has been a welcome guest.

To my writing coach and mentor, Keira Brinton, your vision of voice and impact from the ashes is brilliantly composed and lived. Thank you for your investment in me and this vessel.

To the entire team at JOA Publishing, the work you are engaged in is sacred and connected.

To you, the reader, this book was intended to find you and help you. Thank you for your investment in it. May you find meaningful providence in your life.

ABOUT THE AUTHOR

Art McCracken is a husband, father, mentor, and friend. When he's not working with his clients, you'll find him spending time with his family outdoors or on an adventure behind the lens of his camera.

Known by his clients as the "Executive Whisperer," Art has been an executive mentor for over 20 years. Art's background includes corporate strategy and facilitative work across multiple business sectors. He has served in various board capacities and executive roles within the organizations he has worked with.

Additionally, Art is the Founder and CEO of Snake River Consulting, a highly regarded firm specializing in leadership transformation, growth strategy, and stakeholder engagement, achieving phenomenal results by taking business leaders and their teams to the highest level of performance.

As well as being a published writer, Art is a prolific speaker and educator.

As host of the Honor.The.Gift podcast, Art strongly believes that inspired and intentional leadership is an essential catalyst in building great organizations, and that progressive leaders at all levels can be mentored to create exceptional futures, personally and professionally.

Art's calling is "people experience living true."

NOTES AND INSPIRATION

UNLOCKED: THE BEST VERSION OF YOU

As a way of saying thanks, I'd like to offer you FREE ACCESS to a mini course on how to UNLOCK the best version of you.

In this course I'll share what I learned along the way to help you see more clearly the choice in front of you, and the promise of a connected and meaningful existence, as you courageously learn to live true.

To gain FREE ACCESS, scan the QR Code below to begin your journey:

If you're interested in working with Art, inviting him to speak at one of your events, or becoming part of his UNLOCKED community, please visit:

www.choiceisthegift.com/connect

where you can send him a message or join his community.

Made in the USA
Las Vegas, NV
17 October 2024

97070137R00094